DATING TOOLS

A QUICK GUIDE TO MODERN DATING

Rita Lucas

Dedications

To S. Fields, J. Blunt and W. Bell, thank you for seeing in me what I don't always see in myself. Dr. Brown, your work with me the past two years has given me the strength and mental clarity for this work.

Table of Contents

Preface

As a child, I knew I wanted to be married and have children someday; I expected that someday to be in my 30s. In my early 20s, I found myself in a great relationship with an amazing man who taught me the true meaning of unconditional love. Unfortunately, I was too young to understand or appreciate what that meant. After 4 ½ years, I walked out of the relationship as casually as one walks out of a coffee shop on a Sunday morning. "I want to date other people," I said, and although he was heartbroken, we parted ways. Around the same time this happened, I was also going through another major change. I was wrapping up my final semester for my Bachelors degree and found myself afraid of finally being an adult at 25 who could no longer use school as a crutch. At the urging of my best friend, I signed up for an online dating app so I could meet new people and do exactly what I had set out to do: date. Up until this point, I didn't know what "dating" was outside of what I saw on television and read in articles. It all seemed so fun and carefree, and that was exactly what I was looking for. Dating in my 20s lived up to the hype that I created in my mind. I was having so much fun that the occasional lows that came with dating didn't bother me one bit. I had created a mental timeline as to when I would stop dating casually and start dating seriously, as if it were that easy. In my mind when I was ready, I would meet the one and we would live happily ever after; boy was I wrong. What started out as an adventure seven years ago has become a source of frustration now that I am in my 30s. Once I made the decision to date long term, dating stopped being fun. My standards changed, but the men in my age group who I was attracted to weren't on the same page as I was. Dating Tools came about out of frustration, the frustration that one feels when they're doing everything right but don't seem to be getting the expected results. I had read multiple books and articles, I'd tried different ways of meeting people, and yet I kept finding myself back where I started. It seemed as if the rules of engagement had changed without notice, and I didn't know what was going on. I took a step back and decided to put some of my frustrations down on paper because I had to let people know that they were doing this whole dating thing all wrong. Once I started writing, the frustrations started to melt away. My goal then became to make people aware of what dating is and can be in the modern world. Dating Tools is for people who are making their entrance or reentry into the dating arena. This guide was written to help them navigate some of the things that they may come across. Although the road has been rocky at times, it is a road well traveled without any regrets on my part. Along the way, I've learned a lot of lessons and quite a few things about myself. My dating journey has taken me on an emotional rollercoaster, but it has also created a sense of self-awareness, and for that I am thankful.

SECTION 1:
THE MARKET

Chapter 1

What Is Dating?

The word dating has multiple meanings; it can easily be defined as two people who are interested in each other, who get together to determine if there is a romantic connection. Dating can be two people actively going out and spending time together to build a romantic relationship. Dating can also be two people getting together to explore each other sexually. No matter how you define dating, the bottom line is there is a romantic connection involved, and with that connection comes feelings and expectations. It is essential for anyone wanting to date to be clear about how they define dating and be able to convey that to a potential match. The purpose of this is to avoid getting caught in the web of confusion or disappointment that sometimes comes with dating.

Dating isn't anything new; people have been dating or courting for centuries as a means of finding a wife/husband or companionship. What is new is how people connect and date in modern society. Before embarking on your dating journey, you should be clear about what your objectives are. The modern dating world isn't meant for those who are mentally or emotionally unstable. It is best to be comfortable and secure within yourself before you decide to date, even if you're dating casually. Dating is full of twists and turns and emotional ups and downs. Being unstable and dating opens you up to being taken advantage of or hurt.

Having a clear objective helps tremendously, especially if you're looking to date seriously or looking for something long term. For those looking for something more casual, being clear is also helpful because it prevents you from wasting your time with people who are dating with different intentions.

There are many ways that you can go about making sure that you're ready; it all depends on you. One of the ways you can go about preparing yourself is by making a list. Your list should consist of general or specific things that you want in a person. After your list of wants is complete, you should also make a list of deal-breakers. This list should be as clear as possible so when you are faced with those deal-breakers, you're clear that they are things you're not willing to accept.

Chapter 2

Purposes of Dating

With dating being such a broad spectrum, identifying where you fit in will save you a lot of time, money, and potential heartache. While some people may be looking for something serious like marriage or long-term companionship, others are looking to have fun and casually meet people to date. Although there is no wrong or right way to do this, it is important to make those you meet aware of your intentions early on. There are various reasons why people date. In this chapter, we will discuss three of the main reasons people date.

Casual Dating and Socialization

Dating can and should be fun, depending on how you approach it. Often times, those who date for fun date casually and take advantage of the variety that comes with dating. Those who typically date for fun or socialization also date as an activity or to connect with other like-minded people. The terms and agreement for this type of dating are usually loose and easy because most of

11

the time, a long-term commitment isn't the objective. This is also a great space to date in if you're unsure about what you want out of a relationship. This method of dating enables you to engage or disengage with whomever you want whenever you want without too many restrictions. This realm of dating allows for freedom and exploration with few expectations; it just requires honesty and transparency.

Long-Term or Companionship

Long-term dating or companionship is the goal for most people who date. This form of dating can be a stepping-stone for those patiently waiting for marriage. Looking for Mr. or Mrs. Right can be daunting after a while for some. Some people are not interested in the uncertainty that comes with casual dating and prefer to connect with one person for the long haul. Everyone isn't looking for variety; some are looking for stability. Unlike casual dating, this form of dating comes with lots of expectations and a time commitment. Indulging in long-term dating can be just as fun and exciting as casual dating without the revolving door of potential partners. There are many people who enjoy connecting with someone to discover, nurture, and grow their shared interests into something meaningful. This form of dating requires more work in terms of vetting and compatibility, but it's worth it in the long run. The essential thing to keep in mind is that a long-term partner deserves your time and attention because this is the person you may be waking up to for a while.

Dating for Marriage

Similar to long-term dating, those who are dating for marriage are looking for stability and a life-long commitment. Marriage is a commitment between two people for life. Creating a solid foundation is essential to making this type of relationship work. Matters of the heart can be difficult to navigate at times, hence the reason you should study your partner closely before deciding to marry them. Before committing to the first person who comes along to sweep you off your feet, make sure that the two of you are compatible. Depending on the age of those dating for marriage, things sometimes tend to move quickly. When dating for marriage, it is important to make your intentions clear from the beginning so that your time isn't wasted. People who are dating for marriage are usually very clear about their objective when they enter the dating realm. Your objective shouldn't just be marriage; it should be to find the best person to spend the rest of your life with.

Chapter 3

Classes of Dating

The modern dating world is filled with multiple options for meeting people. No longer are you forced to go to bars and nightclubs or wait to be introduced by someone to meet people. Because of modern technology, you now have the ability and convenience of meeting people in the comfort of your home or by going to a place created for singles searching for a connection with someone. As great as these options are, there are some drawbacks and obstacles, but that is to be expected because everything has its pros and cons.

There are two major classes of dating. These classes are known as traditional and non-traditional dating.

Non-Traditional Dating

Today non-traditional dating seems easier than traditional dating. It's easier in the sense that you can meet anyone within the comforts of your home, and it is easy to engage or disengage at any time, but it has its pros and cons. Let's explore some of the possible ways of meeting in a non-traditional way.

Online Dating

Let's start by jumping into online dating because that is one of the more common ways of meeting people today. Although many people dislike online dating, there are just as many people who embrace it and use online dating platforms to connect with other singles around the world. You should keep in mind that dating online isn't much different from meeting people in your daily life. The truth is you can meet unpleasant characters anywhere. Anyone or anything that you're looking for is available on the online platform; it's just a matter of finding it. There are plenty of dating apps available to choose from. Figure out what works best for you by asking friends and family who have used online dating as a tool. You can also do a little research on Google and see what works best for you based on your list of wants and preferences. Once you've found a few apps that work for you, the next thing to do is to create an account. If you're just starting out, it might be best to start with one app to see what's available and figure out how to navigate the online dating platform. If you're comfortable, you can sign up for a couple of apps to maximize your chances of meeting someone. Some platforms require payment to have full access to the app, but there are a lot of free apps that can get the job done. In the beginning, you might be a little nervous about putting your pictures up and telling "strangers" about yourself, but after a few weeks, some of those jitters should disappear. Once you start meeting people, the first couple of weeks can be nerve-racking and tedious. Sometimes getting past the initial small talk and connecting with someone for a decent and coherent conversation can be frustrating and difficult, but it is vital to keeping the connection alive. One of the dreadful things about online dating is that due to so many options, people are less patient or less likely to put a lot of effort into the initial courting process. You shouldn't let that deter you; give the platform at least a month before moving on. At times the process of maintaining your profile feels like having a second job, but it all becomes worth it when you finally find someone to connect with.

Advantages and Disadvantages
of Online Dating

PRO	CON
Cost-effective: You can meet and connect with people for free because there are a lot of dating apps that allow you to connect without being charged.	**Easier for people to lie or be predatory:** Due to the anonymity that the internet affords us, some people take advantage and are not as truthful as they should be or use it to prey on others.
Accessible and convenient: You can connect anywhere and anytime as long as you have a Wi-Fi connection.	**Fake profiles do exist:** Unfortunately, not everyone who uses online dating has the best intentions. People create fake profiles for many reasons, so be aware that they do exist.
Opportunity to know more about others before connecting: Almost all dating platforms allow you to create a profile where you can write a	**People that you're not interested in will contact you:** Although

synopsis of who you are and what you're looking for. This head start prevents you from wasting time with people you may not be compatible with.

You get to meet people outside of your environment: Online dating gives you access to people who live in other parts of the world or people that you may have never met otherwise.

Multiple options and varieties: There are millions of people online to choose from, and they are all looking for a variety of things. The online dating platform allows you to connect with some of these people.

you may have your filters on, or you're looking for someone in particular, there's always someone looking for you. People that you're not interested in will reach out, and hopefully, they do so in a polite manner. In case they don't, you have the option to block them or report them to the app.

Lack of human interaction: Unlike traditional ways of meeting, this method of connecting prevents you from hearing or physically seeing a person before matching with them. Although pictures are available, they can easily be

Customizable: Most dating apps have a feature where you can select or filter out the types of singles you're looking for. You can tailor your search to fit your ideal mate from height, location, or dating objectives.

First impressions are up to you: You have space and time to create the best first impression by creating a profile that not only stands out but also gives your potential match a real idea of who you are.

doctored and manipulated.

People who misuse the platform: In recent years, dating apps have become a playground for people who are not genuinely interested in finding love. Unfortunately, people are now misusing it to network or meet people platonically.

Can be time-consuming and frustrating: Finding love in real life isn't easy, and online dating is no different. This method requires a lot of time and energy to sift through the numerous apps and profiles to find the one.

Rejection is inevitable: This method doesn't shield you from rejection; it may make it more prevalent. Due to the lack of face-to-face interaction, people are more comfortable ending things abruptly without explanation.

Tip: Create a Gmail account specifically for your online dating profile. Once you've met someone or decide to no longer engage in online dating, it's easier to disable the email address or walk away from it.

Speed Dating

Speed dating is another way to meet people; especially if you live in a major city. The idea behind speed dating is to have a short 5-10-minute date with a number of people in one night. Once the dates are over, you decide if you'd like to see more of the person or people you've met. These events typically take place at a bar or a lounge that has been reserved for the speed dating. They usually have a theme of some sort based on age, ethnicity, careers, etc. This is how it works: The same number of men and women sit across from each other and get to know each other one-on-one until the host of the event rings a bell to signal that the "date" is over and it is time to rotate. Typically, the men will rotate to the next person until everyone in the room has "dated" each other. At the end of the night, you list the names of those you would like to engage further with, and then turn it into the host of the event or log your list of connections on the event's website. If there is a mutual connection, the host will send out a message with the contact information for both parties, or you will get a message from the host directing you to sign in to the website to check your matches. This is usually done within 48 hours or less from when the event took place. You are then left to get in contact with each other at your own leisure. Traditionally, men are expected to make the first move, but that belief has gone out the window for some. I've matched with people while speed dating and never heard from them because now some men want to be chased rather than doing the chasing. Once contact has been made after the event, you should continue working on getting to know the person you matched with and plan an actual first date if the attraction still exists. Because you've already met each other face-to-face and had the opportunity to test if there was any chemistry, working your way towards a first date should be a little easier than if the two of you had met on a dating app.

Advantages and Disadvantages of Speed Dating

PRO	CON
Most people are there for the same reason: People go into speed dating because they are single and looking for a mate. **Committed to the process:** Most people there are serious about finding someone and are clear about conveying that, especially because there	**There is a cost attached:** Although there are many free ways to meet people, this method of connecting isn't one of them. Most speed dating events cost about $20-50. **Not enough time:** Due to the time limitations, it can be challenging to get a good feel for the

is a fee associated with speed dating.

Customizable to an extent: Some speed dating events are general in terms of just having an age requirement, while others can be specific. There are speed dating events that are geared towards people of a certain race or ethnicity, people who are a certain height, people who work in specific industries or careers, etc.

It's just enough time: Because the time you have to converse with someone is limited, it doesn't feel too bad if you're on a "date" with someone and there's no connection. Within a

other person or truly gauge if the person sitting across from you could be the one.

Too many options: Although you are allowed to put down more than one name, it can be difficult to make a decision because of there being so many people to choose from in such a short time frame. Sometimes one date is better than another, and you find yourself torn about what to do.

Some people may look at it as an activity: Although most people who go speed dating are serious, there are a select few who are single and have attended these events to few minutes, you will get another chance at potentially meeting another person that you click with.

Safe environment: Speed dating events take place in a public venue with lots of people present, so there is no need to worry too much about safety.

No pressure to choose: Due to selections being made privately, you don't have to feel pressured to choose someone if there was no connection. They would have no way of knowing you did not select them until the event is over.

say that they've tried speed dating, almost like checking off something on their bucket list.

No guarantees: Because you pre-register for the event, you don't know who will show up or if you will connect with any of the people who do show up. With this being the case, it's possible that you could leave the event without making a love connection.

Tip: Get to the event venue at least 15-20 minutes early so you can grab a drink or get comfortable in the environment. This will help with nerves and allow you to have the best date possible.

Singles Events/Meetup

Singles events such as the ones featured on Meetup are also great ways to meet people. Meetup is a platform that allows everyday people to create groups about things that interest them. Meetup isn't limited to dating; it's available to singles, couples, and those who are looking for platonic connections within their city. Anyone can join or create a group on Meetup based on their interests for free. The way this works is that the organizer of the group will create an event and invite all the members in the group. Although members of the group who RSVP can bring a guest, attending alone is encouraged because it forces you to interact with the people at the event. The events are usually held at bars, lounges, or similar venues that can accommodate the activity at hand. The events vary in size and cost. Some of the events are free, while others require a fee. The idea behind this method of connecting is to put single people from all different walks of life in a room and allow them to connect at their own pace. Some event coordinators facilitate conversations by having icebreakers and other small games throughout the event that enable the attendees to talk to each other, while others let the guests connect on their own. I didn't do too well at my first Meetup event, but don't rule this out as an option. Although I was there to meet other singles, I ended up leaving the event with another woman's number with plans to have lunch. I didn't make a love connection that night or any other night, but it was an experience worth having. These singles events provide a safe environment without any pressure to decide on the spot.

Platonic Meetup Groups

Although Meetup has groups geared towards singles getting together for the sole purpose of dating, there are plenty of Meetup groups that are based on platonic connections. Sometimes getting together with people who share similar interests is a great way to connect and potentially meet the one. This requires you to leave the house and possibly get out of your comfort zone, but it is a great way to connect and make new friends without any pressure. If the theme of the group is something that you genuinely enjoy or are interested in, it makes it easier to spark up a conversation that could lead to something more than a platonic connection. For specified groups, you will often see the same people most of the time, but there are times when groups will collaborate, which opens the pool of people you can meet.

Advantages and Disadvantages of Singles Events/Meetup Groups

PRO	CON
Safe environment: These events take place in a public venue so there is a low risk of danger.	**The ratio of men to women is unpredictable:** You never know who is going to show up to these events, so there is a possibility that there would be more of one sex over the other.
No pressure: While you're there to meet other single people, there is no pressure to connect with anyone unless someone catches your eye.	**There is minimal customization:** Unlike online and speed dating, you don't get to choose what type of singles you'll meet. You
Everyone is invited and can attend: With	

Meetup events, you can bring someone with you if you RSVP for that guest. Because anyone can attend, it opens the possibility for you to meet more people.

The environment is relaxed and casual: Although you're at a singles event, you're only encouraged to have conversations. This is done through icebreakers and games throughout the evening, but once again, there is no pressure to participate if you choose not to.

You get a chance to talk to people for as long as you want to: Since the evening has no real structure, you are free to speak with show up to an event filled with people of all shapes and sizes from all walks of life. Even if you're part of a themed Meetup group, there is still the possibility of there being singles at the event who don't fit the group theme.

Everyone is invited and can attend: There is no vetting process, so you must really engage with the attendees to connect. This can make the process tedious because you may find yourself at an event where there are a lot of people who are not a match for you.

There might be a cost attached: Although there are free events, most singles events cost whomever for as long as you'd like if you're enjoying the conversation.

Good way to meet friends: The platonic meetups are a great way to meet people; especially if you're new to a city.

about $20 or more depending on the activity. Light refreshments and sometimes a drink ticket are included.

Used as a space for networking for some: Unfortunately, there are people at singles events who are there to further their careers aspirations rather than meet a potential partner.

Tip: If you're talking to someone at a singles event and you want to leave, you can excuse yourself to use the bathroom or get another drink. You can also decide to be honest and nicely let them know that you'd like to walk around the room a bit and meet some other people.

Traditional Dating

Unlike online dating and speed dating, traditional dating can be looked at as an old-fashioned way of connecting. Although some consider this dating method to be outdated, it is still used quite often by many people. Traditional dating usually involves two people meeting face-to-face in an organic way. Those who prefer this method of connecting enjoy many advantages.

Bars and Clubs

Meeting someone in the club or a bar is more traditional compared to some of the aforementioned options, though it can still be an effective way to connect with people. Those who are interested in the club scene and like to dance should get out and mingle with other singles in their city. This method of meeting people is another great way to meet people without any pressure. The only thing you are plagued with is finding the right place to hang out for the night. This can quickly be done by getting suggestions from friends or doing a quick Google search. Choosing the right place is important because the night doesn't have to go to waste if you don't connect with someone. This idea also puts you in an environment where you're surrounded by people who are interested in the same type of music or lifestyle that you're into. Although this is an option for meeting people, most people who go to bars and clubs go to have fun with friends and dance. Few people go to bars and clubs alone, so the intent isn't necessarily to meet other singles. However, the opportunity is still there.

Advantages and Disadvantages of Meeting People in a Bar or a Club

PRO	CON
Physical: You get to see the person's physical attributes and determine if there's any chemistry right on the spot. **Fun:** You're in a social environment, dancing, drinking, and having a good time.	**Loud music:** With the music being so loud, it becomes difficult to have a conversation. **Lighting:** The lighting may set a mood for dancing and fun, but it makes it difficult to clearly see faces. **Not fully coherent:** Alcohol consumption

Organic: The conversation is on the spot and natural. It usually continues because both parties are drawn to each other.

A lot of options: There are plenty of people to choose from. Even if you are rejected by one, you still have a chance of potentially meeting someone.

No pressure: The atmosphere is a fun and casual, so you don't have to engage with anyone romantically if you don't want to.

Spontaneous: It's not planned, so there is an element of fun and surprise to everything.

makes it difficult to know if the connection is genuine or not.

Rejection: Although rejection is a part of the dating, it is worse because it is immediate, and face-to-face.

Relationship status: You don't know if the people there are single or just there to party.

Requires resources: Time, effort, and money are necessary because you must go outside of your home to engage.

Limitation: You're limited to people in your city or a specific area.

Hard to find love: Most people may be looking for hook-ups instead of love.

Meeting People in Sports Bars

Sports bars are a great way to meet people who are interested in sports. During any major sport's season, it's easy to walk into a sports bar on game night and be in a room full of people enjoying the game who may be single. For those who don't know anything about sports, you can easily pick a sport and learn enough about it so that you can have a decent conversation with someone who enjoys sports. Being in the right place at the right time is a major part of dating and can increase your chances of potentially meeting someone. This idea isn't unique to sports or bars alone; it can be applied to other interests. The idea behind this is to put yourself in a room full of people whose interests you don't mind learning in hopes of connecting.

Tip: Going to bars by yourself increases your chances of meeting someone. People are more inclined to start a conversation with you if they believe you're alone.

Meeting People in Real Life

Another traditional and effective way to meet people is by meeting them while living life. You encounter people every day when you step outside your home. You can meet people during your commute, at work, while running errands, at the gym, or through a friend or a family member. Although it is a traditional way of meeting people, this method can be full of mystery. It is unlike online dating where you can customize what you want by using filters. With this method, you're left to base your level of interest predominantly on how a person looks or the information that the "matchmaker" shared with you. This method of connecting should not deter you from properly vetting this person. You must be sure that this person is someone who meets your requirements. It can be difficult not to jump in too quickly if you already have prior knowledge or were introduced to someone but do your best not to move too fast. Keep in mind that you must learn who this person is on a romantic level because they may be different from who they are on a platonic level.

Advantages and Disadvantages of Meeting People in Real Life

PRO	CON
Physical: You can see a person's physical attributes and how they move.	**Superficial thoughts:** You could miss out on a great connection due to superficial thoughts — for instance, you not accepting someone's romantic advances because they are not your physical type.
Body language: Body language is very important in determining if there is any chemistry. The way a person looks at you, the faces, and the gestures they make can say a lot about interest.	**Mysterious:** Depending on where you meet them, you may not know anything about them. This can be fine for some people, but for others it can be unsettling.
Personality: Knowing a person before taking that step towards being romantically involved has its benefits. A person's personality can win you over even	**Not customizable:** You don't get to choose a person's attributes

if you weren't initially physically attracted to them.

Tone: You get to hear the tone and inflections in the person's voice.

ahead of time.

Pressure: You might feel pressured to date or entertain someone; especially if a friend or family member introduced you or you regularly see that person.

Awkward: If you connect with someone at work and it doesn't work out, it can be uncomfortable or difficult to see the person regularly.

Great Places to Meet People Traditionally

- Festivals/fairs and cultural events

- The grocery store

- Restaurants, bars, and cafes in your neighbourhood that you regularly visit.

- Go to events and places that interest you alone. (Art shows/galleries, Museums, Live music venues, etc.)
- Volunteer

Chapter 4

Advantages and Disadvantages of Modern Dating

Now that you know some of the different ways that people connect, you now have the option of choosing what works best for you. For those adventurous souls, you should give all the different methods a try and see where you land. Dating as a whole is rarely going to be seamless. Whether you choose the traditional route or the non-traditional route, there will be hurdles you will have to get over. Below are a few general advantages and disadvantages that are associated with modern dating. Don't let any of these things give you pause on your quest to finding the one; instead, be aware that these things might come up and adjust if they do.

PRO	CON
Personality-based matches: It is more	**Untruths:** The online method of modern

encouraging to date someone with the same personality type, interests, or zodiac sign that aligns with yours, rather than linking up with a random person you meet in a bar or café and trying to figure out if you're a match. Modern dating gives you the opportunity to know a person's opinions, likes, and dislikes before jumping in.

Shyness: Those who are not the outgoing type can find it challenging to meet new people traditionally. Modern dating has a platform that allows you to hide behind your computer screen and still connect with people. This gives

dating makes it much easier for individuals to lie about their profiles and themselves. The cute guy you got matched with via a dating site might not be a suicide bomber, but it's possible he's not a 6'2", 27-year-old like he said he was.

Distance: Distance is a considerable barrier to modern dating. It may be easy to find a like-minded person with similar interests with whom you become comfortable with over the course of time. However, if there is distance between the two of you, it can become challenging or stressful trying to maintain a connection

40

you the opportunity to get to know someone and get comfortable with them before meeting them face-to-face.

Passively date: Imagine being able to make love connections while you work or sleep. The online dating platform provides that luxury. Once you've created a profile, you don't have to always tune in for someone to like you or for the two of you to match. This modern dating method allows you to tailor your level of involvement on a whim so it suits your lifestyle.

or to see each other as frequently as you would like.

Incompatibility: It's difficult to conclude on the compatibility of the person you've interacted with online. That engineer you meet online might be exciting and fun to talk to online, but in real life, they may not be as attractive as you thought, or they may exhibit certain mannerisms that you're not fond of.

SECTION 2:
THE DATE

Chapter 5

All You Need to Know About Dating

After exploring all the options available to you, you have now met someone. You've managed to connect with someone and are having enough coherent conversations for you to go on a date. The premise of a date is for you to see if the initial connection and chemistry you experienced over the phone is present now that you're face-to-face. Dating can be scary; especially the first date, but it doesn't have to be as long as you know what you are doing.

It is advisable to wait at least five days or more after connecting with someone before venturing out on a date because it gives you a chance to feel out the other person. It also gives you a chance to properly plan out a date with some idea of what the other person likes rather than planning a generic date that doesn't suit either of you. Blindly going on dates without properly vetting the person via conversation can be a waste of time and money after a while. On the other hand, you shouldn't wait more than four weeks, if time

45

permits, to go out on the first date because you run the risk of having wasted your time if the chemistry you had over the phone doesn't translate into a physical connection.

Before the Date

Appearance

Physically going on a date is an important part of dating. The date could be the end of something that you thought could be wonderful or the beginning of something that you may have been sceptical about. First impressions are hard to forget, so you want to make sure you show up at your best. You should be well-groomed and showered when you arrive. Poor hygiene can be a major turnoff, no matter how great the conversation is. I remember going out on a date with a guy who not only showed up late, but he also showed up looking dishevelled. I had to feign fatigue to get out of the date. Needless to say, there was no second date. Your clothes should be clean and pressed, without any stains, holes, or tears. Dress comfortably but appropriately for the planned activity.

Punctuality

Besides being clean and well put together, punctuality is another important factor in dating. Being on time shows respect for the person that you are meeting. Agreed, life does happen and sometimes you may find yourself running a bit late, but it is important to communicate that to your date. If you believe you will be more than 30 minutes late, reschedule or inform your date and let them make the decision to wait. Because communication is key, if a date is more than 15 minutes late without communicating with you, it is okay to leave the date.

First Date Conversations

First date conversations should be meaningful, but also fun and light. Having a good conversation that flows with someone you're getting to know can be difficult. Although there is no wrong or right way to go about getting to know someone, there are some topics that you should steer clear of or wait until the two of you are better acclimated with each other. Below is a short list to help with the conversation part of the date.

Do's:

- Ask thoughtful questions or questions that you genuinely want to know the answers to.

- Ask questions about their interests and taste (music, movies, and hobbies).

- Ask about career and short-term goals.

- Ask about traveling (where they've gone and maybe want to go).

Don'ts:

- Exes (Try to steer clear of talking about previous relationships, good or bad.)

- Money and finances (No need for either of you to divulge detailed financial information about each other.)

- Sex (There are plenty of other things to discuss besides this, unless this is a casual connection.)

- Don't interrogate (This is a conversation, not 21 questions, it should flow.)

The Date

First dates are always filled with anxiety and butterflies with the added pressure of figuring out where to go, what to do, and how much to spend. A first date is supposed to put you in an environment where the two of you have space and time to converse. Space and time do not require a lot of money spent. Your first date should always be in a public place. You should always make sure that someone is aware that you're going on a date and provide them with your date's contact information. Wherever the two of you decide to go, it should be in a place you're both comfortable going with someone unfamiliar. Some singles are taking the less traditional route of dinner and attempting other methods of dating to save time and money.

Non-Traditional First Date

Dating is still dating, but it has slightly shifted in terms of what constitutes a real first date. Tradition and television have shown us that a date includes dinner and a movie or something along those lines. Dinner and a movie are still a part of dating, but first dates have evolved. A non-traditional first date is layered and doesn't involve a lot of upfront commitment in terms of time and money being spent. This form of dating starts with a low-cost activity that either party can easily walk away from if they find the date lacking the type of connection they anticipated. The layering process is a great way to determine if a mutual connection is there before committing a lot of time and money into a situation that's not going anywhere. You start light and build to something more if the connection is there. Some examples of a layered first date:

- Ice cream or dessert → bowling
- Happy hour (1-2 drinks) → dinner or dancing
- Lunch → walk in the park or happy hour
- Cafe (coffee/tea and a pastry) → museum

The whole idea here is if the first part of the date goes well, it's easy to continue the date by doing something else that allows the two of you to continue to get to know each other. If you realize you are not enjoying the date or you are not connecting with the person, it's easy to end the date without too much time or money being spent.

Early on in my dating journey, I had agreed to go on a more traditional date with someone who I wasn't sure about. We made plans for dinner, drinks and a movie that he purchased tickets for ahead of time. I knew a movie wasn't a good first date activity, but there I was. To add insult to injury, it was a comic book movie that I had no interest in seeing. My date proceeded to talk to me throughout most of the movie and after spending about six hours with this man, I was completely turned off by the end of the evening. I had made the mistake of committing too much of my time upfront.

Traditional First Date

A non-traditional first date isn't meant for everyone or every situation. There are many who enjoy a more traditional date with dinner being at the core along with other activities. This method of dating is excellent for people who have built enough rapport with each other and feel confident and comfortable with their connection. It gives both parties space and time to continue to develop what they've already started before the first date. Although a more traditional date is optimal for two people trying to learn about each other, it can be a bit heavy in terms of a commitment of time and finances for a connection that isn't yet secure.

Who Pays for The Date?

Who pays for the date? That is the age-old question that always comes up. Traditionally men usually ask women out, but that is no longer always the case. The rule is whomever asks for the date usually pays for the date. Typically, the man pays for the first and second date, and the woman should offer to cover the gratuity. By the third date, it is courteous and fair for the woman to offer to pay and be prepared to do so if the man accepts her offer. Splitting the check is always an option, but it can be awkward when the check arrives if this wasn't something that was discussed ahead of time. Also, splitting the check on the first date can create the belief that all future checks are to be split, therefore creating a pattern that one or both parties may not be comfortable with. Wooing or being wooed is an important part of dating, so splitting the check can be one of the many ways to potentially kill a budding romance. It is easier for one person to pay the bill while the other person leaves the gratuity, if necessary. If you're engaging in a non-traditional date, one person can pay for one part of the date while the other pays for the second part. Regardless of who is expected to pay for the date, you should always show up prepared to cover at least your cost of the date in case things don't work out.

Date Two

Once you've made it past the first date and you are comfortable moving forward, it is now time to plan a more substantial date where more time is spent together. With first date jitters out of the way, you can now focus on getting to know the person and be more of yourself. Dinner or a lengthier activity is encouraged at this point because you now know that there is a face-to-face connection, and the feelings shared between the two of you are mutual. Even at this stage, dinner isn't the only option for a more engaging date. There are plenty of other activities that would give you the space and time to explore and discover your date. Below is a list of date ideas that will give you more of an idea of a person's personality than dinner could.

Date ideas for date Two

- Miniature golf, bowling, or pool: this could show you how competitive your date is while having fun.

- Museum (art, history, spy, colour, interactive, etc.): this type of date allows you to have conversations about a multitude of things and test your date's intellect and perspective.

- Escape room: this is a fun way to see if your date is a team player and how they communicate under pressure.

- Sip and paint: this is a way for both of you to showcase your creativity while enjoying each other's company.

SECTION 3:
THE FOLLOW-UP

Chapter 6

Types of Dating

You've made your list and met someone, then you made it through the scary first date and a few other dates. Now what? You would think it's smooth sailing at this point, but now you have a new set of obstacles to face. As time passes and feelings grow, so do expectations. Depending on the type of relationship you're looking for, questions about sex, other partners, or exclusivity may pop up. This is where you must determine if the initial attraction is enough to keep things going.

Casual Dating

With all the different options available to meet people, it's easy to find yourself dating more than one person. In the world of modern dating, this is usually the norm. If you're casually dating, it's understood that you're not looking for anything too serious. It is important that you make those you are dating aware of this so they can decide as to whether this is a situation they are looking for. Although you may not be looking for anything long-term, dating as a whole still requires a lot of your time and energy; that time should be spent with someone who understands the terms and conditions of the situation. When casually dating, you should be forthcoming about the other people you're dating without giving details. Although the conversation stage is where you should clarify what you're looking for, your intentions should be clearly spelled out for all parties involved at this point in the game.

Advantages and Disadvantages of Casual Dating

PRO	CON
Variety: Casual dating gives you access to a lot of different people, which in turn keeps things fun, fresh, and exciting.	**Lack of a go-to person:** One of the cons of casual dating is that you don't have the support that most people in long-term relationships have. You're left to deal with the emotional ups and downs of life on your own.
Full autonomy: Casual dating allows you to do as you please, whenever, wherever and with whomever. You	

are not obligated to anyone; therefore, you don't have to consider anyone else when making decisions.

Experiment: Because casual dating gives you the freedom to meet as many people as you'd like, it makes it easier for you to hone in on the ideal person you may one day want to settle down with.

Easy to disengage: Because you're not in a committed relationship, you don't have to deal with the emotionally heavy stuff that usually comes with relationships. There's no pressure to commit, therefore, when things are no longer working for you, it's easier to

Costly: Dating, in general, is expensive. Casually dating can become costly after a while, especially if you're dating multiple people.

Health and safety: Although casual dating isn't synonymous with casual sex, it does leave the door open for more sexual partners who may not be as careful as you are when engaging with other people. This revolving door of partners could put you more at risk.

Feeling left out: Casually dating and keeping your options open can sometimes leave you feeling left out of couple themed

59

| end things. | events or activities, depending on your circle of friends. |

Tip: I don't suggest you entertain more than three people at a time. Any more than three people at a time makes it challenging to engage and get to know someone. You also run the risk of spreading yourself too thin, trying to keep up with everyone involved.

Long-Term Dating

Everyone approaches dating with different objectives. It can sometimes be difficult to determine where a new romance is going after a few dates. Unlike casual daters, those who are looking to date long-term intend to find someone to grow closer to and grow with. It is important that your intentions are made clear fairly early on to make sure that everyone involved is on the same page. Although making your intentions clear doesn't guarantee a long-term relationship, it does let everyone know that there are expectations. Making a commitment for the long term requires work. Both parties will have to devote time and energy to nurture this budding relationship. This phase is where you hone in on the list that you created to guide you in finding the one. This is also the time when it's important to take your time in learning each other and have fun doing so. As with every partnership, there will be highs and lows, but creating a solid foundation could help to ease some of the futures lows or make them easier to manage.

Advantages and Disadvantages of Long-Term Dating

PRO	CON
Comfortable: One of the great things about long term dating is you have the benefit of knowing who you're dealing with, and you can be your authentic self.	**Lack of excitement:** One downside to long-term dating is it can become routine and boring if both parties get complacent.
Less anxiety: You no longer have to deal with the stress of dating or going through the	**Restricted freedom:** More than likely, you're spending more time with your love interest and less time with your single

feelings of uncertainty that comes with meeting someone new and trying to figure out if they're the one or if you're what they're looking for.

Your health: Once you've made a commitment to each other and gotten tested, you can breathe a sigh of relief knowing that your chances of catching an STD are unlikely due to being monogamous with one person.

You have a shoulder to lean on: A long-term monogamous relationship guarantees you constant support in good and bad times and someone in your corner who cares.

friends. You also have to take someone else's feelings into consideration before making decisions.

Lack of variety: After a while, sex can lose its thrill and become repetitive because it's the same person.

Getting stuck with the wrong person: While looking for stability, you may find yourself stuck with the wrong partner if you don't do your due diligence before committing. Once committed, you may find it difficult to leave because you're comfortable with the person.

The Serious Stuff

Sex

Sex! It's fun, passionate, sensuous, and exciting. It's a significant part of modern dating. Regardless of what your objective is while dating, this topic is something that will definitely come up. Whether you choose to engage or not is up to you; those who wish to engage should do so without any pressure. Boundaries should be clear and mutually understood so everyone involved feels safe and enjoys the act. There is no set timeframe as to when sex should be introduced, but when it is introduced, it becomes an essential factor in developing the connection or a relationship. Sex is so important that it sometimes becomes a determining factor as to whether one should continue dating a person or not. As amazing as sex is and should be, be careful not to introduce it too early unless you're looking to have sex and just date casually. Introducing sex too soon can affect how things move forward. If you have sex too early, and it is as titillating as it should be, it can cloud your judgment. You may find yourself overlooking things you regularly wouldn't allow, perhaps even allowing some of those deal-breakers to slip through. On the other hand, if the sex isn't what you expected, you may find yourself turned off and no longer interested in someone whose company you enjoyed up until that point. Giving yourself and your partner more time to connect outside the bedroom gives you more time to create a mental connection and bond that usually transfers over into the bedroom once you're ready to take that step.

Sexuality

Sexual fluidity is slowly becoming a common thing for modern singles. Although most singles are either heterosexual or homosexual, there are some who are open to experiencing all sides of the sexual spectrum. Men and women are becoming more comfortable with exploring with the same sex as well as pushing the limits with the opposite sex. Modern dating comes with a variety of ways in which people identify with their sexuality. The key thing to remember is to be honest about who you are, but also respect who other people choose to be whether you agree with it or not. Your sexual proclivities and interests should be made clear to your partner when the topic of sex comes up. You should be open and comfortable with talking about your sexual interests as well as open to receiving what your partner has to share about their sexuality. Sex is meant to be enjoyable for all those involved. By not being transparent, you're only preventing yourself from enjoying sex to the fullest.

Exclusive Dating

Dating has many nuances and compartments, exclusive dating falls into one of those many compartments. Exclusivity is a stage that some singles may never experience, while others may find themselves stuck in that stage. The exclusive stage typically comes after several dates and a couple of months of dating. Regardless of whether you're dating casually or seriously, most singles are often dating multiple people. Once you find yourself really connecting with someone, you make a request for exclusivity. This request is made because perhaps one or both parties may not be ready for a full-blown relationship, or they would like to test the waters before jumping into an actual relationship. Exclusivity allows both singles to continue to explore and nurture this newfound bond without the distractions of other people. This may sound like a relationship, but there is a fine line between exclusivity and a relationship. That line is defined by you being introduced either as a boyfriend or girlfriend or just a friend. Because exclusive dating can mean different things to different people, it is very important to be clear about the terms you and your partner have outlined. This ensures there is no confusion and enables you to make a seamless transition into a relationship.

Rejection

When dealing with matters of the heart, rejection or heartbreak is inevitable. Because modern dating comes with a revolving door of potential suitors, the likelihood of rejection is higher and also more frequent. Sometimes the rejection isn't what stings the most; rather, it's the way in which a person decides to end things. "Ghosting" and "curving" have become common terms used to describe how a person chooses to reject you. Unfortunately, I have used these methods to reject people and they have also been used on me. With age and experience, I've realized that it's easier to just have a conversation. You'd be surprised by how receptive people are or can be when you're direct and honest, yet tactful.

Ghosting

No matter how attractive you are or how great of a personality you have, there is always going to be someone looking for something other than what you bring to the table. Because most people use texting or some form of phone communication to get to know the people they are dating, it's easier to disconnect or "ghost" without a word. Rather than have an awkward conversation about no longer being interested, some people would rather drop off the face of the earth. This method of rejection often leaves the ghosted person feeling blindsided because it's often done without explanation or warning.

Curving

As terrible as ghosting sounds, curving is even worse. Rather than just ending things without a word, some would rather drag out the process and string a person along with excuses and lies until the person being "curved" realizes what is going on. This form of rejection often leads to frustration and confusion because the person being curved often doesn't know it's happening until it's too late. Typically curving leads to ghosting, but the residual effects of heartbreak tend to be worse because the person being curved truly believed the broken promises that were made to them at one point.

Signs a Person Isn't Interested:

- Always "busy"- anyone who is interested in you will make time for you no matter how busy of a lifestyle they lead.

- Never initiates outings or time spent together- when someone is interested, they not only take every opportunity to see you, they create opportunities as well.

- Takes a long time to respond to your messages- with everyone's phone readily at their fingertips, it's hard to believe that someone needs hours or days to respond to messages.

- Not attentive- being physically present is one thing, but being emotionally or mentally present is also important. If they keep asking you the same questions over and over, that's a sign that they're not paying attention or listening to you.

- Makes excuses or lies- anyone who makes excuses, doesn't keep their word, or flat out lies about trivial things is not as interested as you may think.

- Doesn't ask you questions about your life and always talks about themselves- that's a sign that they are not only uninterested, but that they may need a therapist, not a partner.

SECTION 4:
TIPS & ADVICE

Chapter 7

Staying Safe

While looking for love, it's easy to find yourself caught up in the whirlwind of it all. No matter what you are out here seeking, your safety should not be sacrificed. Common sense, intuition, and awareness are just some of the things you will have to hone in on while trying to navigate the modern dating world. Below are a few safety guidelines that can help you stay safe while looking for the one.

- **Get a Google Voice number:** Something as simple as a phone number can be used to locate you and other bits of information about you that you may not be ready to share when you first meet someone. One way to connect with someone you've just met is by using a Google Voice number. Google Voice gives you a level of anonymity while still allowing you to message and make voice calls with a phone number that isn't yours.

- **Go public:** Never agree to a first date at someone's house. This is to provide a layer of protection in case the connection isn't there or the person turns out not to be the person you thought they were. Also, a person is less likely to create a scene or try to harm you if you're out in public.

- **No ride sharing:** Find your own way to the first date. You don't want your date knowing where you live in case things don't work out and they become unhinged. Being able to leave the date whenever you're ready to go without depending on someone who you may have just snubbed is also helpful.

- **Have a buddy system:** Always let a friend or a family member know who you're going out with on a first date. Also, set a check-in time for you to communicate with that person to let them know that you're ok.

- **Comfortable shoes:** Being comfortable on a first date is important in more ways than one. Wearing comfortable but appropriate shoes is key in case you need to move swiftly and remove yourself out of a situation.

- **Do your research:** Surprises can be fun, but a first date is not the time for that. Never blindly walk into a date; always research where you're going to make sure that you're comfortable with the space.

- **Don't over commit:** Try not to over commit your time on a first date until you know for sure the connection is there and it's mutual. You will have plenty of time and opportunities to see your date again if the two of you click. There's no need to commit to drinks, dinner, and a show all in one night. Although there's a chance of the date going well, there's also a chance that you would feel compelled to stay even if you're not having a good time because you committed to all these activities ahead of time.

- **Keep your personal information safe:** Never disclose your personal information with anyone that you've just met. Personal information such as detailed workplace information, your home address, certain types of pictures, and financial details should be kept to yourself until you've built a rapport and a certain level of trust with the person.

- **Keep your money to yourself:** Never send anyone that you've met online any money, especially someone that you've never met face-to-face.

- **Be respectful:** Before making any physical advances such as touching, petting, or kissing, make sure that it's wanted. The chemistry between the two of you should suggest that it's ok, but if you're unsure just ask.

- **Intuition:** Always be aware and trust your gut; if it doesn't feel right, it probably isn't right. Do not hesitate to remove yourself from a situation that doesn't feel good.

Whether you are going on your first date or your 15th date, here are some great date ideas that will allow you to continue to grow the bond that you and your partner have created.

Date Ideas

Museums	Movie theatre
Art galleries	Play or musical
Amusement parks	Bike riding
Miniature golf	Festival
Escape room	Comedy show
Sip and paint	Arcade
Picnic in the park	Beer garden or brewery
Concert	Bar or lounge
Dancing	Drive in theatre
Karaoke	Zoo
Drinking on a rooftop	Roller skating

Gourmet bakery	Ice skating
Ice cream	Hiking
Botanical garden	Bowling
Movie in the park	Wine tasting
The beach	Trivia
Picnic	Cidery
Game night	Smoke hookah
Planetarium	City tour
Live sporting event	Shoot pool

Printed in Great Britain
by Amazon

79822266R00047